Park Jobs

by Sascha Goddard

OXFORD
UNIVERSITY PRESS
AUSTRALIA & NEW ZEALAND

What do park helpers do?

Park helpers do lots of jobs in the park.

One part of the job is to help with the plants.

This park helper stops pests from spoiling plants.

He gets rid of weeds that have crept up.

This man helps little brown frogs in the park.

There are not a lot of them now.

He must keep the frogs from harm.

Some parks have lots of sand.

Her job is to fix this twisting trail.
She shifts the driftwood off
the track.

Children come to see this park.

The park helper tells them what to look at.

Then he spends a crisp morning clearing out a trench.

When it rains, soil slips down this embankment.

Trees might come down.

The trunks will drift off in the river.

The park helper plants lots of trees.

This will help to stop the soil slipping.

Some men got stuck in this park.
One man fell down a steep hill.

Park helpers look for them.

They help the men get out of the park.

Park helpers do a lot of jobs.

Parks need them.
We need them, too.